D1180739

Winnie-the-Pooh Telephone Book

A.A. Milne
Illustrated by E.H. Shepard

Methuen Children's Books

This edition published for DMG in 2001
by Methuen Children's Books
an imprint of Egmont Children's Books Limited
239 Kensington High Street, London W8 6SA
Copyright © 1998 Michael John Brown, Peter Janson-Smith,
Roger Hugh Vaughan Charles Morgan and
Timothy Michael Robinson, Trustees of the Pooh Properties.
From *Winnie-the-Pooh* first published 1926 and
The House at Pooh Corner first published 1928
text by A. A. Milne and line illustrations by E. H. Shepard
copyright under the Berne Convention.
Colouring of cover illustrations copyright © 1973 and 1974
Ernest H. Shepard and Methuen Children's Books Ltd.
Design copyright © 1998 Egmont Children's Books Limited.

7 9 10 8 6

ISBN 0 416 19967 4

Printed in China

This book belongs to

....

Useful Addresses

Useful Addresses

Pooh

A   "Rabbit," said Pooh to himself. "I *like* talking to Rabbit. He talks about sensible things. He doesn't use long, difficult words, like Owl. He uses short, easy words, like 'What about lunch?' and 'Help yourself, Pooh.' I suppose, *really*, I ought to go and see Rabbit."

Name

Address

Tel   Fax

Mobile

E-mail

Name

Address

Tel   Fax

Mobile

E-mail

Name

Address

Tel   Fax

Mobile

E-mail

A

But he hadn't got far before he began to say to himself:
"Yes, but suppose Rabbit is out?"
"Or suppose I get stuck in his front door again, coming out,
as I did once when his front door wasn't big enough?"
"Because I *know* I'm not getting fatter,
but his front door may be getting thinner."

Name

Address

Tel   Fax

Mobile

E-mail

Name

Address

Tel   Fax

Mobile

E-mail

Name

Address

Tel   Fax

Mobile

E-mail

Name

Address

Tel   Fax

Mobile

E-mail

A

Name

Address

Tel   Fax

Mobile

E-mail

Name

Address

Tel   Fax

Mobile

E-mail

Name

Address

Tel   Fax

Mobile

E-mail

Name

Address

Tel   Fax

Mobile

E-mail

Name

Address

Tel   Fax

Mobile

E-mail

A

Name

Address

Tel   Fax

Mobile

E-mail

Name

Address

Tel   Fax

Mobile

E-mail

Name

Address

Tel   Fax

Mobile

E-mail

Name

Address

Tel   Fax

Mobile

E-mail

Name

Address

Tel   Fax

Mobile

E-mail

B And all the time . . . he was going
more and more westerly,
without thinking . . . until suddenly he
found himself at his own front door again.
And it was eleven o'clock.
Which was Time-for-a-little-something. . . .

Name

Address

Tel   Fax

Mobile

E-mail

Name

Address

Tel   Fax

Mobile

E-mail

Name

Address

Tel   Fax

Mobile

E-mail

B

Name

Address

Tel   Fax

Mobile

E-mail

Name

Address

Tel   Fax

Mobile

E-mail

Name

Address

Tel   Fax

Mobile

E-mail

Name

Address

Tel   Fax

Mobile

E-mail

Half an hour later he was doing what he had always
really meant to do, he was stumping off to Piglet's house.

Piglet was busy digging a small hole in the
ground outside his house.

B

Name

Address

Tel   Fax

Mobile

E-mail

Name

Address

Tel   Fax

Mobile

E-mail

Name

Address

Tel   Fax

Mobile

E-mail

Name

Address

Tel   Fax

Mobile

E-mail

Name

Address

Tel   Fax

Mobile

E-mail

"I'm planting a haycorn, Pooh, so that it can
grow up into an oak-tree, and have lots of haycorns
just outside the front door instead of having to
walk miles and miles, do you see, Pooh?"

Name

Address

Tel   Fax

Mobile

E-mail

Name

Address

Tel   Fax

Mobile

E-mail

Name

Address

Tel   Fax

Mobile

E-mail

Name

Address

Tel   Fax

Mobile

E-mail

B

Name

Address

Tel   Fax

Mobile

E-mail

Name

Address

Tel   Fax

Mobile

E-mail

Name

Address

Tel   Fax

Mobile

E-mail

Name

Address

Tel   Fax

Mobile

E-mail

Name

Address

Tel   Fax

Mobile

E-mail

B

Name

Address

Tel   Fax

Mobile

E-mail

Name

Address

Tel   Fax

Mobile

E-mail

Name

Address

Tel   Fax

Mobile

E-mail

Name

Address

Tel   Fax

Mobile

E-mail

Name

Address

Tel   Fax

Mobile

E-mail

C

"Well," said Pooh, "if I plant a
honeycomb outside my house, then it
will grow up into a beehive."

"Or a *piece* of honeycomb . . .
Only then I might only get a piece of a beehive,
and it might be the wrong piece, where the bees
were buzzing and not hunnying. Bother."

Name _____

Address _____

_____

_____

Tel _____ Fax _____

Mobile _____

E-mail _____

Name _____

Address _____

_____

_____

Tel _____ Fax _____

Mobile _____

E-mail _____

Name _____

Address _____

_____

_____

Tel _____ Fax _____

Mobile _____

E-mail _____

C

Name

Address

Tel   Fax

Mobile

E-mail

"Besides, Pooh, it's a very difficult thing, planting unless
you know how to do it," he said; and he put the acorn in the
hole he had made, and covered it up with earth, and jumped on it.

When Piglet had finished jumping, he wiped his paws on his front,
and said, "What shall we do now?" and Pooh said,
"Let's go and see Kanga and Roo and Tigger," . . .
So they set off . . .

Name

Address

Tel   Fax

Mobile

E-mail

Name

Address

Tel   Fax

Mobile

E-mail

Name

Address

Tel   Fax

Mobile

E-mail

Name

Address

_C_

Tel   Fax

Mobile

E-mail

Name

Address

Tel   Fax

Mobile

E-mail

Name

Address

Tel   Fax

Mobile

E-mail

Name

Address

Tel   Fax

Mobile

E-mail

Name

Address

Tel   Fax

Mobile

E-mail

C

Name

Address

Tel   Fax

Mobile

E-mail

Name

Address

Tel   Fax

Mobile

E-mail

Name

Address

Tel   Fax

Mobile

E-mail

Name

Address

Tel   Fax

Mobile

E-mail

Name

Address

Tel   Fax

Mobile

E-mail

D   "Look, Pooh!" said Piglet suddenly.
"There's something in one of the Pine Trees."
"So there is!" said Pooh, looking up wonderingly.
"There's an Animal."

Piglet took Pooh's arm, in case Pooh was frightened.
"Is it One of the Fiercer Animals?" he said, looking the other way.

Name

Address

Tel   Fax

Mobile

E-mail

Name

Address

Tel   Fax

Mobile

E-mail

Name

Address

Tel   Fax

Mobile

E-mail

D

Name

Address

Tel   Fax

Mobile

E-mail

Name

Address

Tel   Fax

Mobile

E-mail

Pooh nodded.
"It's a Jagular," he said.

"They hide in the branches of trees and drop on
you as you go underneath," said Pooh.
"Christopher Robin told me."

Name

Address

Tel   Fax

Mobile

E-mail

Name

Address

Tel   Fax

Mobile

E-mail

Name

Address

Tel   Fax

Mobile

E-mail

Name

Address

Tel   Fax

Mobile

E-mail

Name

Address

Tel   Fax

Mobile

E-mail

Name

Address

Tel   Fax

Mobile

E-mail

Name

Address

Tel   Fax

Mobile

E-mail

D

Name

Address

Tel   Fax

Mobile

E-mail

Name

Address

Tel   Fax

Mobile

E-mail

Name

Address

Tel   Fax

Mobile

E-mail

Name

Address

Tel   Fax

Mobile

E-mail

Name

Address

Tel   Fax

Mobile

E-mail

E

"Help! Help!" it called.
"That's what Jagulars always do,"
said Pooh, much interested.
"They call 'Help! Help!' and then when you
look up, they drop on you."

"I'm looking *down*," cried Piglet loudly, so as the Jagular
shouldn't do the wrong thing by accident.

Name

Address

Tel   Fax

Mobile

E-mail

Name

Address

Tel   Fax

Mobile

E-mail

Name

Address

Tel   Fax

Mobile

E-mail

E

Name

Address

_____

Tel   Fax

Mobile

E-mail

Name

Address

Tel   Fax

Mobile

E-mail

Name

Address

Tel   Fax

Mobile

E-mail

Name

Address

Tel   Fax

Mobile

E-mail

Name

Address

Tel   Fax

Mobile

E-mail

Something very excited next to the Jagular heard him, and squeaked:
"Pooh and Piglet! Pooh and Piglet!"

All of a sudden Piglet felt that it was a much nicer day
than he had thought it was. All warm and sunny —
"Pooh!" he cried. "I believe it's Tigger and Roo!"
"So it is," said Pooh. "I thought it was a Jagular and another Jagular."

E

Name

Address

Tel   Fax

Mobile

E-mail

Name

Address

Tel   Fax

Mobile

E-mail

Name

Address

Tel   Fax

Mobile

E-mail

Name

Address

Tel   Fax

Mobile

E-mail

E

Name

Address

Tel   Fax

Mobile

E-mail

Name

Address

Tel   Fax

Mobile

E-mail

Name

Address

Tel   Fax

Mobile

E-mail

Name

Address

Tel   Fax

Mobile

E-mail

Name

Address

Tel   Fax

Mobile

E-mail

F   "We can't get down, we can't get down!" cried Roo.
"Isn't it fun? Pooh, isn't it fun, Tigger and I
are living in a tree, like Owl, and we're going to stay
here for ever and ever. I can see Piglet's house.
Piglet, I can see your house from here. Aren't we high?
Is Owl's house as high up as this?"

Name

Address

Tel   Fax

Mobile

E-mail

Name

Address

Tel   Fax

Mobile

E-mail

Name

Address

Tel   Fax

Mobile

E-mail

Name

Address

Tel   Fax

Mobile

E-mail

F

"Piglet," said Pooh solemnly, when he had heard all this,
"what shall we do?" And he began to eat Tigger's sandwiches.
"Are they stuck?" asked Piglet anxiously.

"Couldn't you climb up to them?"
"I might, Piglet, and I might bring Roo down on my back,
but I couldn't bring Tigger down. So we must think of
something else." And in a thoughtful way
he began to eat Roo's sandwiches, too.

Name

Address

Tel   Fax

Mobile

E-mail

Name

Address

Tel   Fax

Mobile

E-mail

Name

Address

Tel   Fax

Mobile

E-mail

Name

Address

Tel   Fax

Mobile

E-mail

Name

Address

Tel   Fax

Mobile

E-mail

Name

Address

Tel   Fax

Mobile

E-mail

Name

Address

Tel   Fax

Mobile

E-mail

Name

Address

Tel   Fax

Mobile

E-mail

F

Name

Address

Tel   Fax

Mobile

E-mail

Name

Address

Tel   Fax

Mobile

E-mail

Name

Address

Tel   Fax

Mobile

E-mail

Name

Address

Tel   Fax

Mobile

E-mail

Name

Address

Tel   Fax

Mobile

E-mail

G . . . he had just got to the last but one when there was a crackling in the bracken, and Christopher Robin and Eeyore came strolling along together.
"I shouldn't be surprised if it hailed a good deal to-morrow," Eeyore was saying. "Blizzards and what-not."

Name

Address

Tel   Fax

Mobile

E-mail

Name

Address

Tel   Fax

Mobile

E-mail

Name

Address

Tel   Fax

Mobile

E-mail

G

Name

Address

Tel   Fax

Mobile

E-mail

Name

Address

Tel   Fax

Mobile

E-mail

Name

Address

Tel   Fax

Mobile

E-mail

Name

Address

Tel   Fax

Mobile

E-mail

Name

Address

Tel   Fax

Mobile

E-mail

Name _____

Address _____

_____

Tel _____ Fax _____

Mobile _____

E-mail _____

Name _____

Address _____

_____

Tel _____ Fax _____

Mobile _____

E-mail _____

Name _____

Address _____

_____

Tel _____ Fax _____

Mobile _____

E-mail _____

"It's Christopher Robin!" said Piglet. "*He'll* know what to do."

"*I* thought," said Piglet earnestly,
"that if Eeyore stood at the bottom of the tree,
and if Pooh stood on Eeyore's back,
and if I stood on Pooh's shoulders —"

G

Name

Address

Tel   Fax

Mobile

E-mail

Name

Address

Tel   Fax

Mobile

E-mail

Name

Address

Tel   Fax

Mobile

E-mail

Name

Address

Tel   Fax

Mobile

E-mail

Name

Address

Tel   Fax

Mobile

E-mail

H "I've got an idea!"
cried Christopher Robin suddenly.
"Listen to this, Piglet," said Eeyore,
"and then you'll know what we're trying to do."

Name

Address

Tel   Fax

Mobile

E-mail

Name

Address

Tel   Fax

Mobile

E-mail

Name

Address

Tel   Fax

Mobile

E-mail

H

Name

Address

Tel   Fax

Mobile

E-mail

Name

Address

Tel   Fax

Mobile

E-mail

Name

Address

Tel   Fax

Mobile

E-mail

Name

Address

Tel   Fax

Mobile

E-mail

"I'll take off my tunic and we'll each hold a corner, and then
Roo and Tigger can jump into it, and it will be all soft
and bouncy for them, and they won't hurt themselves."
"*Getting Tigger down*," said Eeyore, "and *Not hurting anybody*.
Keep those two ideas in your head, Piglet, and you'll be all right."

Name

Address

Tel   Fax

Mobile

E-mail

Name

Address

Tel   Fax

Mobile

E-mail

Name

Address

Tel   Fax

Mobile

E-mail

Name

Address

Tel   Fax

Mobile

E-mail

Name

Address

Tel   Fax

Mobile

E-mail

H

H

Name

Address

Tel   Fax

Mobile

E-mail

Name

Address

Tel   Fax

Mobile

E-mail

Name

Address

Tel   Fax

Mobile

E-mail

Name

Address

Tel   Fax

Mobile

E-mail

Name

Address

Tel   Fax

Mobile

E-mail

I When Roo understood what he had to do,
he was wildly excited . . . and he jumped –
straight into the middle of the tunic.
And he was going so fast that he bounced up again
almost as high as where he was before . . .

But Tigger was holding on to the branch . . .
"Just wait a moment," said Tigger nervously.
"Small piece of bark in my eye."
And he moved slowly along his branch.

Name

Address

Tel   Fax

Mobile

E-mail

Name

Address

Tel   Fax

Mobile

E-mail

Name

Address

Tel   Fax

Mobile

E-mail

Name

Address

Tel   Fax

Mobile

E-mail

Name

Address

Tel   Fax

Mobile

E-mail

I

"Come on, it's easy!" squeaked Roo.
And suddenly Tigger found how easy it was.
"Ow!" he shouted as the tree flew past him.

Name

Address

Tel   Fax

Mobile

E-mail

Name

Address

Tel   Fax

Mobile

E-mail

Name

Address

Tel   Fax

Mobile

E-mail

Name

Address

Tel   Fax

Mobile

E-mail

Name

Address

Tel   Fax

Mobile

E-mail

Name

Address

Tel   Fax

Mobile

E-mail

Name

Address

Tel   Fax

Mobile

E-mail

I

Name

Address

Tel   Fax

Mobile

E-mail

Name

Address

Tel   Fax

Mobile

E-mail

Name

Address

Tel   Fax

Mobile

E-mail

Name

Address

Tel   Fax

Mobile

E-mail

Name

Address

Tel   Fax

Mobile

E-mail

There was a crash, and a tearing noise, and a confused
heap of everybody on the ground.
Christopher Robin and Pooh and Piglet picked
themselves up first, and then they picked Tigger up,
and underneath everybody else was Eeyore.

Name

Address

Tel   Fax

Mobile

E-mail

Name

Address

Tel   Fax

Mobile

E-mail

Name

Address

Tel   Fax

Mobile

E-mail

Name

Address

Tel   Fax

Mobile

E-mail

Name

Address

Tel   Fax

Mobile

E-mail

J

Name

Address

Tel   Fax

Mobile

E-mail

Name

Address

Tel   Fax

Mobile

E-mail

Name

Address

Tel   Fax

Mobile

E-mail

Name

Address

Tel   Fax

Mobile

E-mail

Eeyore said nothing for a long time.
And then he said: "Is Tigger there?"
Tigger was there, feeling Bouncy again already.
"Yes," said Christopher Robin. "Tigger's here."
"Well, just thank him for me," said Eeyore.

J

Name

Address

Tel   Fax

Mobile

E-mail

Name

Address

Tel   Fax

Mobile

E-mail

Name

Address

Tel   Fax

Mobile

E-mail

J

Name

Address

Tel   Fax

Mobile

E-mail

Name

Address

Tel   Fax

Mobile

E-mail

Name

Address

Tel   Fax

Mobile

E-mail

Name

Address

Tel   Fax

Mobile

E-mail

Name

Address

Tel   Fax

Mobile

E-mail

Name

Address

Tel   Fax

Mobile

E-mail

J

Name

Address

Tel   Fax

Mobile

E-mail

Name

Address

Tel   Fax

Mobile

E-mail

Name

Address

Tel   Fax

Mobile

E-mail

Name

Address

Tel   Fax

Mobile

E-mail

Name

Address

Tel   Fax

Mobile

E-mail

Name

Address

Tel   Fax

Mobile

E-mail

Name

Address

Tel   Fax

Mobile

E-mail

Name

Address

Tel   Fax

Mobile

E-mail

K It rained and it rained and it rained.
Piglet told himself that never in all his life,
and *he* was goodness knows *how* old – three,
was it, or four? – never had he seen so much rain.
Days and days and days.

"If only," he thought, as he looked out of the window,
"I had been in Pooh's house, or Christopher Robin's house,
or Rabbit's house when it began to rain,
then I should have had Company all this time . . .

Name _____

Address _____

_____

_____

Tel _____ Fax _____

Mobile _____

E-mail _____

Name _____

Address _____

_____

_____

Tel _____ Fax _____

Mobile _____

E-mail _____

Name

Address

Tel   Fax

Mobile

E-mail

Name

Address

Tel   Fax

Mobile

E-mail

K

Name

Address

Tel   Fax

Mobile

E-mail

Name

Address

Tel   Fax

Mobile

E-mail

Name

Address

Tel   Fax

Mobile

E-mail

Name

Address

Tel   Fax

Mobile

E-mail

Name

Address

Tel   Fax

Mobile

E-mail

Name

Address

Tel   Fax

Mobile

E-mail

K

. . . it wasn't much good having anything exciting like floods,
if you couldn't share them with somebody.

The little dry ditches in which Piglet had nosed
about so often had become streams, the little streams
across which he had splashed were rivers, and the river . . .
had sprawled out of its own bed and was taking up
so much room everywhere, that Piglet was beginning to
wonder whether it would be coming into *his* bed soon.

Name

Address

Tel   Fax

Mobile

E-mail

Name

Address

Tel   Fax

Mobile

E-mail

Name

Address

Tel   Fax

Mobile

E-mail

K

Name

Address

Tel   Fax

Mobile

E-mail

Name

Address

Tel   Fax

Mobile

E-mail

Name

Address

Tel   Fax

Mobile

E-mail

L "It's a little Anxious," he said to himself, "to be a
Very Small Animal Entirely Surrounded by Water."

Then suddenly he remembered a story which
Christopher Robin had told him about a
man on a desert island who had written something
in a bottle and thrown it into the sea . . .

Name

Address

Tel   Fax

Mobile

E-mail

Name

Address

Tel   Fax

Mobile

E-mail

Name

Address

Tel   Fax

Mobile

E-mail

HELP!
PIGLIT (ME)
and on the other side:
IT'S ME PIGLIT, HELP HELP!

. . . and he threw the bottle as far as he could throw
– *splash!* – . . . and he watched it floating slowly away
in the distance, until his eyes ached with looking . . .

Name

Address

Tel   Fax

Mobile

E-mail

Name

Address

Tel   Fax

Mobile

E-mail

Name

Address

Tel   Fax

Mobile

E-mail

Name

Address

Tel   Fax

Mobile

E-mail

L

Name

Address

Tel   Fax

Mobile

E-mail

Name

Address

Tel   Fax

Mobile

E-mail

Name

Address

Tel   Fax

Mobile

E-mail

Name

Address

Tel   Fax

Mobile

E-mail

Name

Address

Tel   Fax

Mobile

E-mail

L

Name

Address

Tel   Fax

Mobile

E-mail

Name

Address

Tel   Fax

Mobile

E-mail

Name

Address

L

Tel   Fax

Mobile

E-mail

Name

Address

Tel   Fax

Mobile

E-mail

Name

Address

Tel   Fax

Mobile

E-mail

M When the rain began Pooh was asleep.

You remember how he
discovered the North Pole;
well, he was so proud of this that he asked
Christopher Robin if there were any other Poles
such as a Bear of Little Brain might discover.

. . . so Pooh went out to discover the East Pole . . .
Whether he discovered it or not, I forget;
but he was so tired when he got home that,
in the very middle of his supper . . .
he fell fast asleep in his chair, and slept and slept and slept.

Name

Address

Tel   Fax

Mobile

E-mail

Name

Address

Tel   Fax

Mobile

E-mail

M

Name

Address

Tel   Fax

Mobile

E-mail

Name

Address

Tel   Fax

Mobile

E-mail

Name

Address

Tel   Fax

Mobile

E-mail

Name

Address

Tel   Fax

Mobile

E-mail

Name

Address

Tel   Fax

Mobile

E-mail

Name

Address

Tel   Fax

Mobile

E-mail

Name

Address

Tel   Fax

Mobile

E-mail

Then suddenly he was dreaming. He was
at the East Pole, and it was a very cold pole
with the coldest sort of snow and ice all over it.

He had found a beehive to sleep in,
but there wasn't room for his legs,
so he had left them outside.

M

Name

Address

Tel   Fax

Mobile

E-mail

Name

Address

Tel   Fax

Mobile

E-mail

M

Name

Address

Tel   Fax

Mobile

E-mail

Name

Address

Tel   Fax

Mobile

E-mail

Name

Address

Tel   Fax

Mobile

E-mail

Name

Address

Tel   Fax

Mobile

E-mail

Name

Address

Tel   Fax

Mobile

E-mail

N And Wild Woozles, such as inhabit the
East Pole, came and nibbled all the fur
off his legs to make Nests for their Young.
And the more they nibbled,
the colder his legs got, until suddenly
he woke up with an *Ow!* –

. . . and there he was, sitting in his chair with his
feet in the water, and water all around him!

Name

Address

Tel   Fax

Mobile

E-mail

Name

Address

Tel   Fax

Mobile

E-mail

Name

Address

Tel   Fax

Mobile

E-mail

Name

Address

Tel   Fax

Mobile

E-mail

Name

Address

Tel   Fax

Mobile

E-mail

Name

Address

Tel   Fax

Mobile

E-mail

Name

Address

Tel   Fax

Mobile

E-mail

"This is Serious," said Pooh. "I must have an Escape."
So he took his largest pot of honey . . .

. . . and when the whole Escape was finished,
there was Pooh sitting on his branch,
dangling his legs, and there, beside him,
were ten pots of honey. . . .

Name

Address

Tel   Fax

Mobile

E-mail

Name

Address

Tel   Fax

Mobile

E-mail

Name

Address

Tel   Fax

Mobile

E-mail

Name

Address

Tel   Fax

Mobile

E-mail

Name

Address

Tel   Fax

Mobile

E-mail

Name

Address

Tel   Fax

Mobile

E-mail

Name

Address

Tel   Fax

Mobile

E-mail

Name

Address

Tel   Fax

Mobile

E-mail

Name

Address

Tel   Fax

Mobile

E-mail

N

O Two days later, there was Pooh, sitting
on his branch, dangling his legs, and there,
beside him, were four pots of honey. . . .

Three days later, there was Pooh,
sitting on his branch, dangling his legs,
and there beside him, was one pot of honey.

Name

Address

Tel   Fax

Mobile

E-mail

Name

Address

Tel   Fax

Mobile

E-mail

Name

Address

Tel   Fax

Mobile

E-mail

Name _____

Address _____

_____

_____

Tel _____ Fax _____

Mobile _____

E-mail _____

. . . it was on the morning of the fourth day that
Piglet's bottle came floating past him, and with one
loud cry of "Honey!" Pooh plunged into the water . . .

"Bother!" said Pooh, as he opened it. "All that wet for nothing.
What's that bit of paper doing?"

Name _____

Address _____

_____

_____

Tel _____ Fax _____

Mobile _____

E-mail _____

O

Name _____

Address _____

_____

_____

Tel _____ Fax _____

Mobile _____

E-mail _____

Name _____

Address _____

_____

_____

Tel _____ Fax _____

Mobile _____

E-mail _____

Name

Address

Tel   Fax

Mobile

E-mail

Name

Address

Tel   Fax

Mobile

E-mail

Name

Address

Tel   Fax

Mobile

E-mail

Name

Address

Tel   Fax

Mobile

E-mail

Name

Address

Tel   Fax

Mobile

E-mail

O

O

Name

Address

Tel   Fax

Mobile

E-mail

Name

Address

Tel   Fax

Mobile

E-mail

Name

Address

Tel   Fax

Mobile

E-mail

Name

Address

Tel   Fax

Mobile

E-mail

Name

Address

Tel   Fax

Mobile

E-mail

P "It's a Missage," he said to himself, "that's what it is.
And that letter is a 'P,' . . . and 'P' means 'Pooh,'
so it's a very important Missage to me, and I
can't read it. I must find Christopher Robin . . .
Only I can't swim. Bother!"

Name

Address

Tel   Fax

Mobile

E-mail

Name

Address

Tel   Fax

Mobile

E-mail

Name

Address

Tel   Fax

Mobile

E-mail

P

So he took his biggest jar, and corked it up.
"All boats have to have a name," he said,
"so I shall call mine *The Floating Bear*."

Christopher Robin lived at the very top of the Forest.

Every morning he went out with his umbrella and put a stick
in the place where the water came up to, and every next morning
he went out and couldn't see his stick any more . . .

Name _____

Address _____

_____

_____

Tel _____ Fax _____

Mobile _____

E-mail _____

Name _____

Address _____

_____

_____

Tel _____ Fax _____

Mobile _____

E-mail _____

Name _____

Address _____

_____

_____

Tel _____ Fax _____

Mobile _____

E-mail _____

P

Name

Address

Tel   Fax

Mobile

E-mail

Name

Address

Tel   Fax

Mobile

E-mail

Name

Address

Tel   Fax

Mobile

E-mail

Name

Address

Tel   Fax

Mobile

E-mail

P

Name

Address

Tel   Fax

Mobile

E-mail

Name

Address

Tel   Fax

Mobile

E-mail

Name

Address

Tel   Fax

Mobile

E-mail

Name

Address

Tel   Fax

Mobile

E-mail

Name

Address

Tel   Fax

Mobile

E-mail

Name

Address

Tel   Fax

Mobile

E-mail

P

Q On the morning of the fifth day he saw the water all round him, and knew that for the first time in his life he was on a real island.

It was on this morning that Owl came flying over the water to say "How do you do?" to his friend Christopher Robin.

Name _____

Address _____

_____

Tel _____ Fax _____

Mobile _____

E-mail _____

Name _____

Address _____

_____

Tel _____ Fax _____

Mobile _____

E-mail _____

Name _____

Address _____

_____

Tel _____ Fax _____

Mobile _____

E-mail _____

Q

Name

Address

Tel   Fax

Mobile

E-mail

Name

Address

Tel   Fax

Mobile

E-mail

Name

Address

Tel   Fax

Mobile

E-mail

Name

Address

Tel   Fax

Mobile

E-mail

Name

Address

Tel   Fax

Mobile

E-mail

Name

Address

Tel   Fax

Mobile

E-mail

Name

Address

Tel   Fax

Mobile

E-mail

Name

Address

Tel   Fax

Mobile

E-mail

"The atmospheric conditions have been very
unfavourable lately," said Owl.

"However, the prospects are rapidly becoming more
favourable. At any moment —"
"Have you seen Pooh?"

Q

Name

Address

Tel   Fax

Mobile

E-mail

Name

Address

Tel   Fax

Mobile

E-mail

Name

Address

Tel   Fax

Mobile

E-mail

Name

Address

Tel   Fax

Mobile

E-mail

Name

Address

Q

Tel   Fax

Mobile

E-mail

Name

Address

Tel   Fax

Mobile

E-mail

R

"Oh, Pooh!" cried Christopher Robin.
"Where *are* you?"
"Here I am," said a growly voice behind him.

"I had a Very Important Missage sent me
in a bottle, and owing to having got some water in my eyes,
I couldn't read it, so I brought it to you. On my boat."

Name _____

Address _____

_____

_____

Tel _____ Fax _____

Mobile _____

E-mail _____

Name _____

Address _____

_____

_____

Tel _____ Fax _____

Mobile _____

E-mail _____   *R*

Name _____

Address _____

_____

_____

Tel _____ Fax _____

Mobile _____

E-mail _____

Name

Address

Tel   Fax

Mobile

E-mail

Name

Address

Tel   Fax

Mobile

E-mail

Name

Address

Tel   Fax

Mobile

E-mail

Name

Address

R

Tel   Fax

Mobile

E-mail

Name

Address

Tel   Fax

Mobile

E-mail

"Isn't there anything about Pooh in it?" asked Bear,
looking over his shoulder.

"Oh, are those 'P's' piglets? I thought they were poohs."
"We must rescue him at once!"

Name

Address

Tel   Fax

Mobile

E-mail

Name

Address

Tel   Fax

Mobile

E-mail

Name

Address

Tel   Fax

Mobile

E-mail

Name

Address

Tel   Fax

Mobile

E-mail

R

Name

Address

Tel   Fax

Mobile

E-mail

Name

Address

Tel   Fax

Mobile

E-mail

"Now then, Pooh," said Christopher Robin, "where's your boat?"

"I ought to say," explained Pooh as they walked down to the shore
of the island, "that it isn't just an ordinary sort of boat. Sometimes it's
a Boat, and sometimes it's more of an Accident. It all depends."
"Depends on what?"
"On whether I'm on top of it or underneath it."

R

Name

Address

Tel   Fax

Mobile

E-mail

Name

Address

Tel   Fax

Mobile

E-mail

Name

Address

Tel   Fax

Mobile

E-mail

Name

Address

Tel   Fax

Mobile

E-mail

Name

Address

Tel   Fax

Mobile

E-mail

Name

Address

Tel   Fax

Mobile

E-mail

Name

Address

Tel   Fax

Mobile

E-mail

R

Name

Address

Tel   Fax

Mobile

E-mail

Name

Address

Tel   Fax

Mobile

E-mail

Name

Address

Tel   Fax

Mobile

E-mail

Name

Address

Tel   Fax

Mobile

E-mail

Name

Address

Tel   Fax

Mobile

E-mail

R

S It wasn't what Christopher Robin expected,
and the more he looked at it, the more he thought
what a Brave and Clever Bear Pooh was, and . . .
the more Pooh looked modestly down his nose
and tried to pretend he wasn't.

Name

Address

Tel   Fax

Mobile

E-mail

Name

Address

Tel   Fax

Mobile

E-mail

Name

Address

Tel   Fax

Mobile

E-mail

"But it's too small for two of us," said Christopher Robin sadly.
"Three of us with Piglet."

Name _____

Address _____

_____

Tel _____ Fax _____

Mobile _____

E-mail _____

Name _____

Address _____

_____

Tel _____ Fax _____

Mobile _____

E-mail _____

Name _____

Address _____

_____

Tel _____ Fax _____

Mobile _____

E-mail _____

Name _____

Address _____

_____

Tel _____ Fax _____

Mobile _____

E-mail _____

S

And then this Bear, Pooh Bear . . . said something so clever
that Christopher Robin could only look at him with mouth
open and eyes staring, wondering if this was really the
Bear of Very Little Brain whom he had known and loved so long.
"We might go in your umbrella," said Pooh.

"I shall call this boat *The Brain of Pooh*," said Christopher Robin,
and *The Brain of Pooh* set sail forthwith in a
south-westerly direction, revolving gracefully.

Name

Address

Tel   Fax

Mobile

E-mail

Name

Address

Tel   Fax

Mobile

E-mail

Name

Address

Tel   Fax

Mobile

E-mail

Name

Address

Tel   Fax

Mobile

E-mail

S

Name

Address

Tel   Fax

Mobile

E-mail

. . . – well, you can imagine Piglet's joy when
at last he saw the good ship, *Brain of Pooh*,
(*Captain*, C. Robin; *1st Mate*, P. Bear)
coming over the sea to rescue him. . . .

Name

Address

Tel   Fax

Mobile

E-mail

S

Name

Address

Tel   Fax

Mobile

E-mail

Name

Address

Tel   Fax

Mobile

E-mail

Name

Address

Tel   Fax

Mobile

E-mail

Name

Address

Tel   Fax

Mobile

E-mail

Name

Address

Tel   Fax

Mobile

E-mail

Name

Address

Tel   Fax

Mobile

E-mail

S

Name

Address

Tel   Fax

Mobile

E-mail

Name

Address

Tel   Fax

Mobile

E-mail

Name

Address

Tel   Fax

Mobile

E-mail

Name

Address

S

Tel   Fax

Mobile

E-mail

Name

Address

Tel   Fax

Mobile

E-mail

T The Piglet lived in a very grand
house in the middle of a beech-tree, and the
beech-tree was in the middle of the Forest,
and the Piglet lived in the middle of the house.

Name _____

Address _____

_____

Tel _____ Fax _____

Mobile _____

E-mail _____

Name _____

Address _____

_____

Tel _____ Fax _____

Mobile _____

E-mail _____

Name _____

Address _____

_____

Tel _____ Fax _____

Mobile _____

E-mail _____

Name

Address

Tel   Fax

Mobile

E-mail

Name

Address

Tel   Fax

Mobile

E-mail

Name

Address

Tel   Fax

Mobile

E-mail

Name

Address

Tel   Fax

Mobile

E-mail

Name

Address

Tel   Fax

Mobile

E-mail

T

Name _____

Address _____

_____

_____

Tel _____ Fax _____

Mobile _____

E-mail _____

Name _____

Address _____

_____

_____

Tel _____ Fax _____

Mobile _____

E-mail _____

Name _____

Address _____

_____

_____

Tel _____ Fax _____

Mobile _____

E-mail _____

Name _____

Address _____

_____

_____

Tel _____ Fax _____

Mobile _____

E-mail _____

T

Next to his house was a piece of broken board which had:
"TRESPASSERS W" on it. When Christopher Robin asked
the Piglet what it meant, he said it was his grandfather's
name, and had been in the family for a long time.

. . . his grandfather had had two names in case he lost one . . .

Name

Address

Tel   Fax

Mobile

E-mail

Name

Address

Tel   Fax

Mobile

E-mail

Name

Address

Tel   Fax

Mobile

E-mail

Name

Address

Tel   Fax

Mobile

E-mail

T

Name

Address

Tel   Fax

Mobile

E-mail

U One fine winter's day when Piglet was
brushing away the snow in front of his house,
he happened to look up, and there was
Winnie-the-Pooh. Pooh was walking round and
round in a circle, thinking of something else,
and when Piglet called to him, he just went on walking.
"Hallo!" said Piglet, "What are *you* doing?"

Name
Address

Tel   Fax
Mobile
E-mail

Name
Address

Tel   Fax
Mobile
E-mail

"Tracking something," said Winnie-the-Pooh very mysteriously.
"Tracking what?" said Piglet, coming closer.
"That's just what I ask myself. I ask myself, What?"

Name

Address

Tel   Fax

Mobile

E-mail

Name

Address

Tel   Fax

Mobile

E-mail

Name

Address

Tel   Fax

Mobile

E-mail

Name

Address

Tel   Fax

Mobile

E-mail

Name

Address

Tel   Fax

Mobile

E-mail

U

Name

Address

Tel   Fax

Mobile

E-mail

"Now, look there." He pointed to the ground in front of him.
"What do you see there?"
"Tracks," said Piglet. "Paw-marks."
He gave a little squeak of excitement.
"Oh, Pooh! Do you think it's a – a – a Woozle?"

Name

Address

Tel   Fax

Mobile

E-mail

Name

Address

Tel   Fax

Mobile

E-mail

Name

Address

Tel   Fax

Mobile

E-mail

U

Name

Address

Tel   Fax

Mobile

E-mail

Name

Address

Tel   Fax

Mobile

E-mail

Name

Address

Tel   Fax

Mobile

E-mail

Name

Address

Tel   Fax

Mobile

E-mail

U

Name

Address

Tel   Fax

Mobile

E-mail

V "What's the matter?" asked Piglet.
"It's a very funny thing," said Bear,
"but there seem to be *two* animals now.
This – whatever-it-was – has been joined by another –
whatever-it-is – and the two of them are now proceeding
in company. Would you mind coming with me, Piglet,
in case they turn out to be Hostile Animals?"

. . . So off they went together.

Name

Address

Tel   Fax

Mobile

E-mail

Name

Address

V

Tel   Fax

Mobile

E-mail

Name _____

Address _____

_____

_____

Tel _____ Fax _____

Mobile _____

E-mail _____

Name _____

Address _____

_____

_____

Tel _____ Fax _____

Mobile _____

E-mail _____

Name _____

Address _____

_____

_____

Tel _____ Fax _____

Mobile _____

E-mail _____

There was a small spinney of larch-trees just here,
and it seemed as if the two Woozles, if that is what
they were, had been going round this spinney;
so round this spinney went Pooh and Piglet after them . . .

Name _____

Address _____

_____

_____

Tel _____ Fax _____

Mobile _____

E-mail _____

V

Name

Address

Tel   Fax

Mobile

E-mail

Name

Address

Tel   Fax

Mobile

E-mail

Name

Address

Tel   Fax

Mobile

E-mail

Name

Address

Tel   Fax

Mobile

E-mail

Name

Address

Tel   Fax

Mobile

E-mail

V

Name _____

Address _____

_____

_____

Tel _____ Fax _____

Mobile _____

E-mail _____

Name _____

Address _____

_____

_____

Tel _____ Fax _____

Mobile _____

E-mail _____

Name _____

Address _____

_____

_____

Tel _____ Fax _____

Mobile _____

E-mail _____

Name _____

Address _____

_____

_____

Tel _____ Fax _____

Mobile _____

E-mail _____

Suddenly Winnie-the-Pooh stopped,
and pointed excitedly in front of him. "*Look!*"
"*What?*" said Piglet, with a jump.
And then, to show that he hadn't been frightened,
he jumped up and down once or twice more
in an exercising sort of way.
"The tracks!" said Pooh.
"*A third animal has joined the other two!*"

V

 "It is either Two Woozles and one,
as it might be, Wizzle, or Two,
as it might be, Wizzles and one, if so it is,
Woozle. Let us continue to follow them."

Name

Address

Tel   Fax

Mobile

E-mail

Name

Address

Tel   Fax

Mobile

E-mail

Name

Address

Tel   Fax

Mobile

E-mail

W

X

Name

Address

Tel   Fax

Mobile

E-mail

And then, all of a sudden, Winnie-the-Pooh stopped again,
and licked the tip of his nose in a cooling manner, for he was
feeling more hot and anxious than ever in his life before.
There were four animals in front of them!

There were the tracks; crossing over each other here,
getting muddled up with each other there; but,
quite plainly every now and then, the tracks of four sets of paws.

Name

Address

Tel   Fax

Mobile

E-mail

Name

Address

Tel   Fax

Mobile

E-mail

Name

Address

Tel   Fax

Mobile

E-mail

Name _____

Address _____

_____

_____

Tel _____ Fax _____

Mobile _____

E-mail _____

Name _____

Address _____

_____

_____

Tel _____ Fax _____

Mobile _____

E-mail _____

Name _____

Address _____

_____

_____

Tel _____ Fax _____

Mobile _____

E-mail _____

"I *think*," said Piglet, when he had licked the tip
of his nose too, and found that it brought very little
comfort, "I *think* that I have just remembered
something . . . that I forgot to do yesterday
and shan't be able to do tomorrow."

Name _____

Address _____

_____

_____

Tel _____ Fax _____

Mobile _____

E-mail _____

W

Name

Address

Tel   Fax

Mobile

E-mail

Name

Address

Tel   Fax

Mobile

E-mail

Name

Address

Tel   Fax

Mobile

E-mail

Name

Address

Tel   Fax

Mobile

E-mail

Name

Address

W

Tel   Fax

Mobile

E-mail

X Pooh looked up at the sky, and then,
as he heard the whistle again, he looked up
into the branches of a big oak-tree,
and then he saw a friend of his.
"It's Christopher Robin," he said.

"Ah, then you'll be all right," said Piglet.
"You'll be quite safe with *him*. Good-bye,"
and he trotted off home as quickly as he could,
very glad to be Out of All Danger again.

Name _____

Address _____

_____

_____

Tel _____ Fax _____

Mobile _____

E-mail _____

Name _____

Address _____

_____

_____

Tel _____ Fax _____

Mobile _____

E-mail _____

Name

Address

Tel   Fax

Mobile

E-mail

Name

Address

Tel   Fax

Mobile

E-mail

Name

Address

Tel   Fax

Mobile

E-mail

Name

Address

Tel   Fax

Mobile

E-mail

Name

Address

Tel   Fax

Mobile

E-mail

X

Y Christopher Robin came slowly down his tree.
"Silly old Bear," he said, "what *were* you doing?
First you went round the spinney twice by
yourself, and then Piglet ran after you and you
went round again together, and then you were
just going round a fourth time —"

"I see now," said Winnie-the-Pooh.
"I have been Foolish and Deluded," said he,
"and I am a Bear of No Brain at All."

Name	
Address	

Tel	Fax
Mobile	
E-mail	

Name	
Address	

Tel	Fax
Mobile	
E-mail	

Y

Z

Name

Address

Tel   Fax

Mobile

E-mail

Name

Address

Tel   Fax

Mobile

E-mail

Name

Address

Tel   Fax

Mobile

E-mail

Name

Address

Tel   Fax

Mobile

E-mail

Name

Address

Tel   Fax

Mobile

E-mail

Y

Z "You're the Best Bear in All the World,"
said Christopher Robin soothingly.
"Am I?" said Pooh hopefully. And then
he brightened up suddenly.
"Anyhow," he said, "it is nearly Luncheon Time."
So he went home for it.

Name

Address

Tel   Fax

Mobile

E-mail

Name

Address

Tel   Fax

Mobile

E-mail

Name

Address

Tel   Fax

Mobile

E-mail

Name

Address

Tel   Fax

Mobile

E-mail

Name

Address

Tel   Fax

Mobile

E-mail

Name

Address

Tel   Fax

Mobile

E-mail

Name

Address

Tel   Fax

Mobile

E-mail

Name

Address

Tel   Fax

Mobile

E-mail

Z